MW00799662

MEDITATION
COLOR BY NUMBERS

MEDITATION
COLOR BY NUMBERS

SIRIUS

This edition published in 2021 by Sirius Publishing, a division of
Arcturus Publishing Limited,
26/27 Bickels Yard, 151–153 Bermondsey Street,
London SE1 3HA

ISBN: 978-1-3988-0897-3
CH008593NT
Supplier 29, Date 0321, Print run 10901

Printed in China

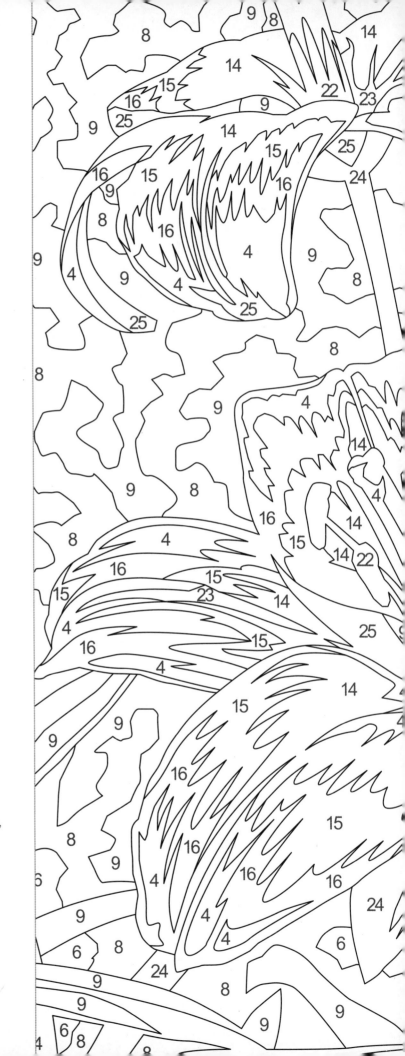

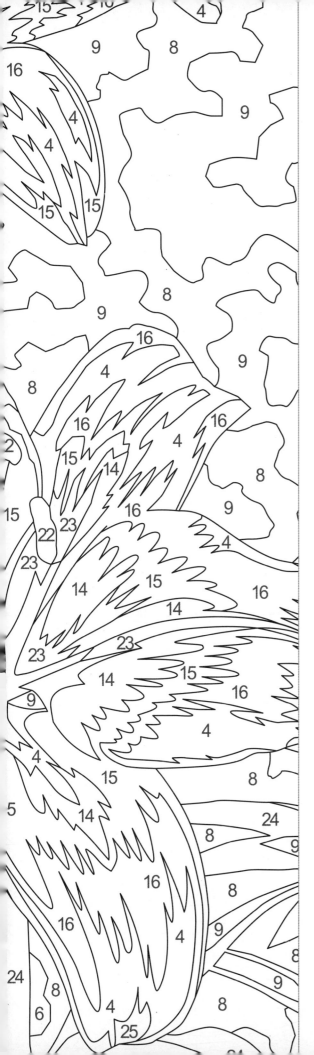

Introduction

Meditation is a very effective way to combat stress and anxiety. It can help to clear your mind and re-establish a sense of calm.

Focusing on an activity, such as coloring in an image, is a great way to begin meditating – the step-by-step creation of a beautiful picture can help anyone to achieve a sense of peace.

The selection of images in this collection has been made with just this aim. In the pages that follow, you will find scenes that remind us of the beauty of the world and the wonderful, natural things in it, plus mandalas, works of art, and soothing, rhythmic patterns.

Whether you follow the colors recommended in the key on the inside back flap of this book, or decide to select your own, you can produce a deeply personal and pleasing set of images.

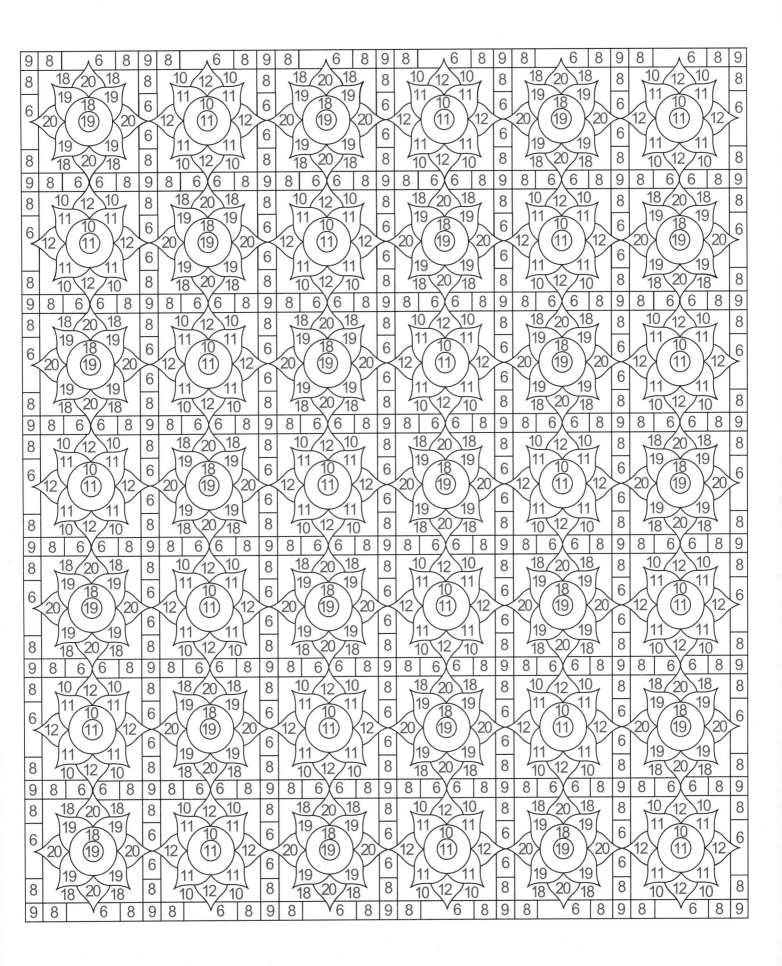

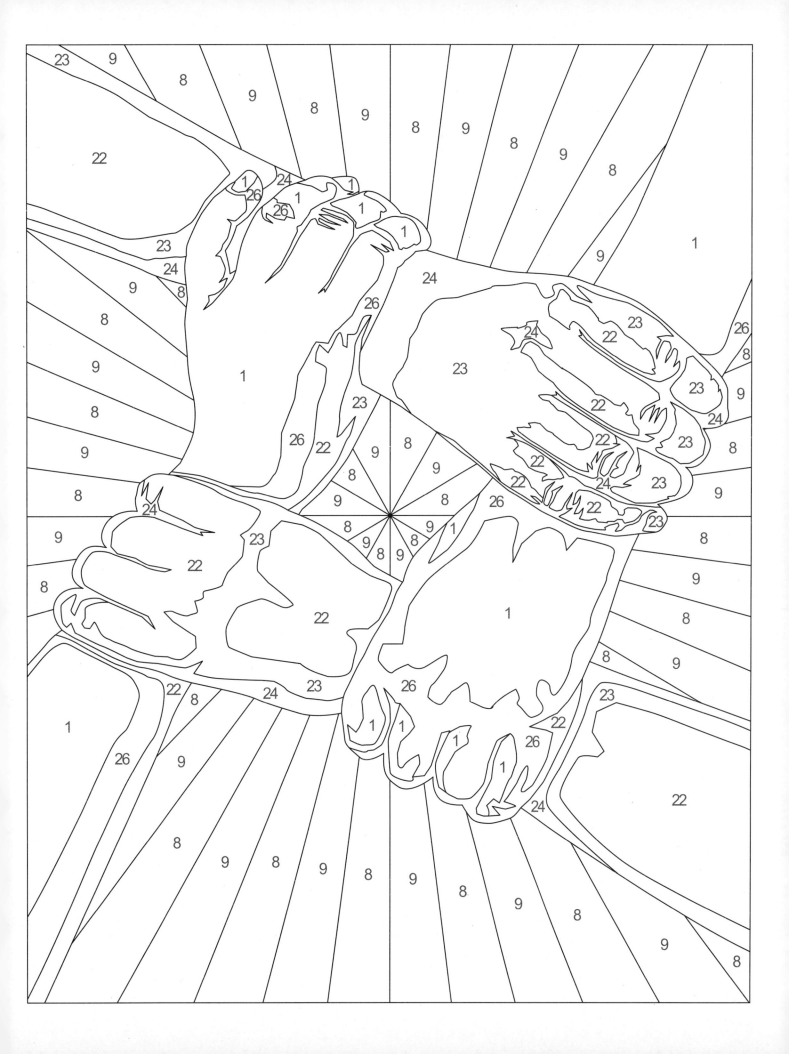

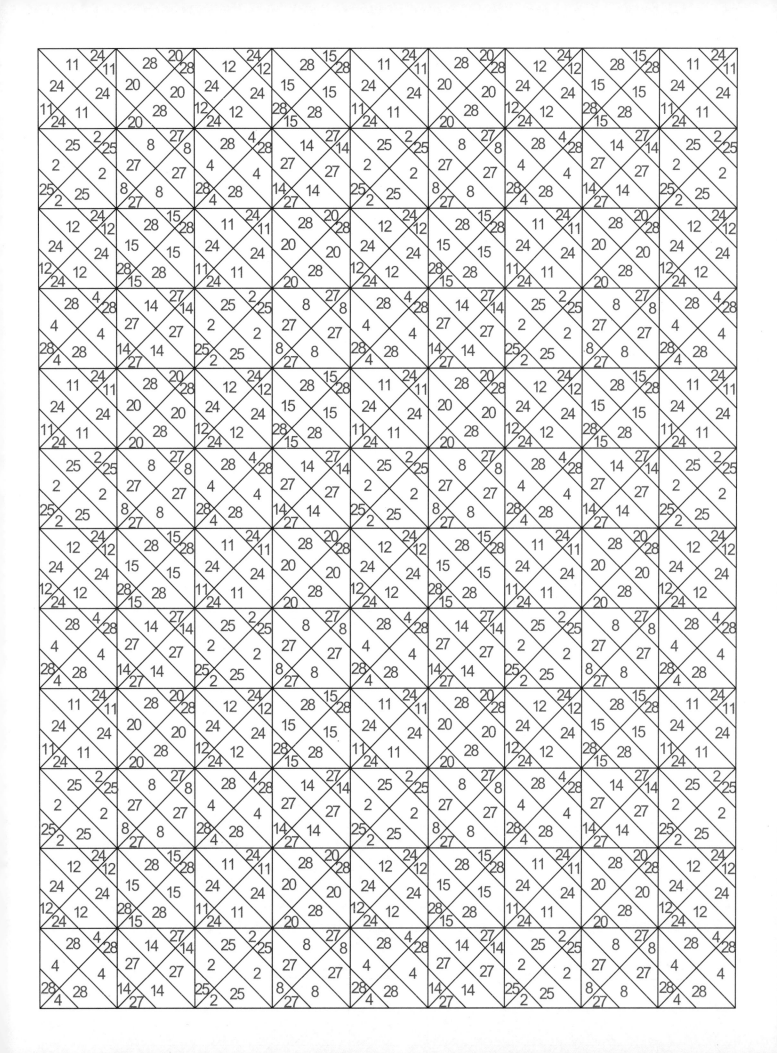

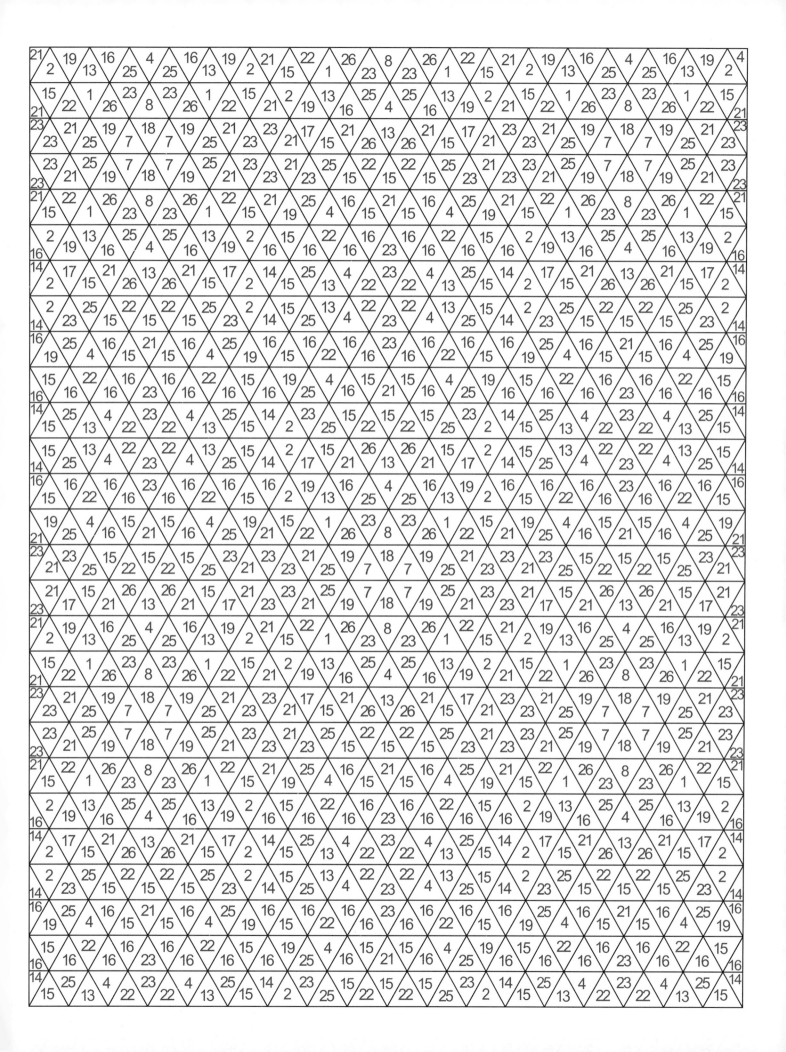